MW00380190

THE SPECIMEN'S APOLOGY

the specimen's apology
Poetry: Copyright © 2019 by George Abraham
Interior artwork: Copyright © 2019 by Leila Abdelrazaq
Cover art by Jasmine Bell. Used by permission of the artist.

Sibling Rivalry Press, LLC
PO Box 26147
Little Rock, AR 72221
info@siblingrivalrypress.com
www.siblingrivalrypress.com

ISBN: 978-1-943977-92-5

By special invitation, this title is housed permanently in the Rare Books and Special Collections Vault of the Library of Congress.

First Sibling Rivalry Press Edition, January 2019

THE SPECIMEN'S APOLOGY

POEMS BY **GEORGE ABRAHAM**

ART BY **LEILA ABDELRAZAQ**

SIBLING RIVALRY PRESS
DISTURB / ENRAPTURE
LITTLE ROCK / ARKANSAS

ACKNOWLEDGMENTS

I would like to thank the following publications where poems from this manuscript have previously appeared:

Poem-a-Day from the Academy of American Poets – "Essay on Submission"

Anomaly – "memory study with specimen in dark universe," "memory study with specimen as lighthouse, in spacetime continuum," "memory study with specimen as apocalypse," and "memory study with specimen at baptism" (published as "Infinite: a history of parallel bodies")

the Blueshift Journal – "[counter/terrorism]"

Boston Review – "the specimen's Lexicon, with Auto-Translate" (published as part of "Cartographies of Wind")

Cosmonauts Avenue – "Post-Script: Against Consolidation" (published as "Against Consolidation" – winner of *Cosmonauts Avenue*'s 2018 Poetry Prize as selected by Tommy Pico)

Kweli Journal – "binary."

LitHub – "ars poetica with parallel dimensions" (published as part of the Nakba 70 Folio)

Mizna (Volume 18.2) – "the specimen's Lexicon with Auto-Translate" (published as "Lexicon") and "the specimen's index" (published as "Index for the damned")

Mizna (Volume 19.2 – the Palestine Issue) – "ars poetica in which every pronoun is a Free Palestine"

Nashville Review – "memory study, in fragmented reality" (published as "portrait of reality, in fragments")

Puerto del Sol – "in which the specimen attempts to define an algebraic structure for their inherited traumas" (both pieces)

the Rumpus – "on unraveling" and "maqam of moonlight, for the wandering"

the Shade Journal – "symposium for the body"

Tin House – "the specimen's apology"

Washington Square Review – "maqam of moonlight, for the children of exile" (both pieces)

Additional thanks to *The Racist Sandwich* podcast and *SlamFind* for publishing recordings of poems from this manuscript, as well as *Stoked Words: An Anthology of Queer Poetry from the Capturing Fire Slam & Summit* for reprinting poems from this chapbook.

First and foremost, I would like to thank Leila Abdelrazaq for illustrating this chapbook and Jasmine Bell for painting this beautiful cover art—no one else could bring these poems to life with art like you two. Second, to Bryan Borland and Seth Pennington and everyone else at Sibling Rivalry Press for the tremendous amount of love and care this project was given. Third, to my heroes, Hala Alyan, Kaveh Akbar, and Tommy Pico, for being among the biggest influences of this project and for having faith in my work.

I'd like to thank my family for their faith in me, especially Jared Abraham (my brother by blood and by choice), Julian Randall (my whole heart and loveliest love, without whom this project literally wouldn't exist), and the rest of my chosen family, namely Noor Ibn Najam, Cat Véléz, Marwa Helal, Hazem Fahmy, Noel Quiñones, Jess Rizkallah, and all my batatas. To torrin a. greathouse, Hazem Fahmy, Marwa Helal, Noor Ibn Najam, Addy Novy, and Natalie Eilbert for shaping the editorial vision of this collection. To my RAWI, Mizna, PYM, and Arab Lit family, namely Randa Jarrar, Farid Matuk, Kamelya Omayma Youssef, Phil Metres, Sara Yasin, Zaina Alsous, Hayan Charara, Peter Twal, Adam Hamze, Noor Hindi, Lena Khalaf Tuffaha, Safia Elhillo, Deema Shehabi, Nader Helmy, Ruth Awad, Sonia Ali, Lana Barkawi, Glenn Shaheen, Tariq Luthun, Jess Abughattas, Summer Farah, and so many more batatas who have shaped and defined me as a poet. To my Kundiman family, especially my 2018 retreat cohort and faculty—my poetry wouldn't be the same without you all. To the Watering Hole and Poetry Foundation Incubator fellows and faculty for reshaping what poetry and community mean to me. To my Boston poetry family, namely Bradley Trumpfheller, RebeccaLynn, Anna Binkovitz, Kayti Lahsaiezadeh, Brandon Melendez, and all members of the Northbeast and Philadelphia slam poetry communities (namely through OASIS, UMB Slam, House Slam, The Boston Poetry Slam, and FEMS). To my mentors, Vision, Dilruba Ahmed, JC Todd, and the Creative Writing departments of Swarthmore and Bryn Mawr College for shaping my voice and helping build the landscape of this project.

To all Palestinians and the homes we build in the diaspora, despite.

CONTENTS

ars poetica with waning memory
after Tarfia Faizullah

> "Even in the highest form of truth, to access memory is to blunder its event."
> — Natalie Eilbert

there was a dead tree rotting behind the church
over there. & wedding bells. they dance. or was it collision
i wanted. the pianist's misstruck chords. a false minor.
he asked what my hands could do. he called me
a dog. it was a joke. he drops the dog. then kisses it. he wanted
me. an *it* he joked about raping. because he could not
admit. it happened. the basement. there. the lights flickering.
until they weren't. an inhabited dark. a being. burnt their soft
coils. i didn't want to. see. anything. his hand sliding
beneath me. pretending he wanted me. to cum. i came
on my own accord. i was never there. my stain, a small country
he didn't notice. i, a small country on his couch. i fled.
i thanked him. on the way out. that language without
a voice. that body without. a dead tree. a rotting.
a man was here once. i pluck the instrument until
no man. o tenor hum. o vibrato of shedding dead.
yes i touched the copper-gutted socket. there was a puddle
5 inches to my left. were i to move. or were it a larger stain
i would have unbroken that circuit &. a light. alight. i flicker. & am
no longer. i touched a white man. once. i do not touch white men
like that. white men touch me like rotting tree. white men fuck me
into dead country. stain on rubble. stain on earthly stain. there were
trees here once. those men's hands stained with its gold. an ethnic
cleansing. i touch myself & do not leak gold. i touch myself. there.
the mind craves. the body cannot. i synapse & closed circuit. desire's
molecular inception. i, expulsion of spinning orbitals. the mind's
momentum. electric. until the body cannot be. until the body, red
& leak. wound un-cauterized. i've killed myself many times. i haven't
died yet. i've died for men. many times. they do not call me
savior. i don't know this song. the words don't translate. the melody,
a pianist's trembling hands. or was it dancing. i familiar the wind. that wind,
a kind of language. you can touch. the language escapes me.

In the video game Bioshock Infinite, *the main character is a man named Booker, who must travel through different realities to find Elizabeth, who has the power to open holes in the space-time continuum and travel between parallel universes.*

The game begins in a reality where Elizabeth is confined in a dark tower which drains her powers. She is guarded by a metallic beast (the Songbird) in order to be studied as a specimen—and later brainwashed—by Comstock, the dictator of their society.

Comstock is revealed to be a version of Booker who, in an alternate reality, has had a spiritual awakening after being baptized. Ultimately, Elizabeth traps all copies of Booker and Comstock into the cosmic instant of the baptism and drowns them, thus freeing herself (and the infinite parallel copies of herself) from this cycle of abuse and trauma.

In all realities, Booker arrives at Elizabeth by traveling through a lighthouse.

This is a history of parallel bodies.

memory study with ~~Elizabeth~~ specimen in dark universe

in the beginning, there was
the body. a *you*, finite enough
to reside, compact, in the confines
of space & time—
                   but before there was
a you, there was the empty. that resides strong
in the body. a longing. a definition—can the body
exist without the Loneliness it counters
               & inhabits—

yes—the Loneliness grew strong within
you. made a world of you, dark
& vast as the beast that guards it;
became a copper-lunged thing;
a thing that sings without breathing,
strips the music from your little
bones; winged beast of metallic
claw & its anthem of shredding wire:
all the delicate machinery built
to contain you—

but in this reality, you are tame
& young. small. hollow
-boned, yet shatterproof in all
your oblivious histories.

you cannot know the way you split galaxies
with a single breath; the universes
your hands can unlock in a single strike—
your history, a petty matchbox that ignites
with friction & hands, always the hands;

you are oblivious of the scientists
behind the screens, who claim
they built you; observing the specimen
of you—who built a tower in you,
the Lonely that makes you retreat
into yourself; who wrote the books
you could never find yourself in; books
that claim they saved you & built all
the delicate machinery & winged
beasts that strip you of flight & sweet
entropy;
           wingless child—
                 the body is an infinity
                 you have yet to unravel—

binary.

once i had a body & that body was a [male/female] body. some days i contoured & dressed the [male/female] body & others i spat it out like a pit or seed uprooted from a digestible flesh. in either case it was a [consumable/indigestible] body. something to swallow & fill the void of every [rapist/lover]. how the body turned [solid/fluid] in the presence of bone-shattering shear & chaotic tensors. how it puddled in its own redaction & swelled, stubborn, much like the blood who cannot unknow the turbulence it was born into. sometimes the body feared its own [male/female] reflection, bestial like only a [terrorist/freedom-fighter] can know. the wrong historian refuses to call my body [occupier/occupied]—says the truth is somewhere in between, is non-binary, but i can think of no [conflict/occupation] more clear than that of this body & isn't that worth a decisive history? no, my gender is not a refugee caught between the ash of two genocides. i cannot be in exile from a body i was [never/always] home in. i only know how to love the body in [fragments/categories]. my gender is a runaway ghost train. my gender is the mirror speaking back in shattered tongues. i am all of the question marks in your medical books. a [doctor/anthropologist] once tried to encode the body into a binary rivulet—a sequence of 0s and 1s to name this digitized fluidity. but even in its purest form, the body was still a mistranslation of itself

you are used to being the only Palestinian ~~boy~~ thing in the room. the only ~~boy~~ thing to call elephant. or beast. you are one

of two in your incoming class of STEM students. the other dropped out in the first week. she was brown, much like your mother. much like a scorched Arab woman. white women scream of exclusion

from science as your family's women are martyred by it. science says your people are the human shields & yet are still the ones beneath the bombs labeled "battle tested." *progress* is collaborating with the scientists making an open-air prison out of your country & calling it experimentation. or habitation. or maybe it was just

survival. you exist at the intersection of these mutations: the aftermath of whatever wars you write your body into. this same science builds the binaries you can never escape: human/subject. occupier/occupied. your people waking up to white phosphorous for sunrise/your people not waking up at all.

***

Implementation of Dynamic Tracking Algorithms on UAV Drones [1]

Abstract: This study involved the design and implementation of control and computer vision algorithms for the detection and tracking of human subjects by unmanned aerial vehicles. Vision methods include image segmentation and supervised learning via artificial neural networks. Our system first splices enemy subjects into a series of deformable visual fields and then uses previously trained databases[2] to inform the identification process. Control schemes include nonlinear architectures for the most robust results. Our system demonstrated fatal accuracy and precision, including object collision detection. Future experimentation involves integrating obstacle aversion algorithms as well as facial detection[3] within the control architecture. Our nation's defense is a top research priority, in this ever-expansive war on Terror, [4] demonstrating an increasing need for such studies.[5]

¹ This project was funded by the US Department of Defense and the US Air Force.
² To avoid conflicts of interest & ~~generate funding~~, research staff
~~& human subjects~~ were primarily scientists of color.
³ Innately *American*.
⁴ Look at how far Affirmative Action has gotten you.
⁵ ~~These are merely the realities we simulate.~~

***

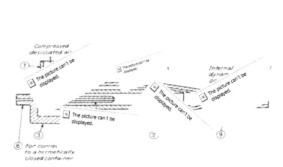

when he invented a laser mechanism that could be used as a weapon of mass destruction, Tesla hid his discoveries from the world. burned the schematics of his death ray and died alone and penniless: the cost of saving the world from his science.

***

white ~~political~~ scientist comes to campus & every specimen turns its back in protest. he says his research proves a genetic superiority of whites based purely on IQ. calls poverty a *genetic* burden & the specimens stand steady as a wall might, as a ~~prison~~ cell might & isn't that *political*? says trump's election was the *poor* white man's burden & it was, at that moment, as silent as election day on campus: when all logic failed us; gravity weighing thick & ungodly; us, amoeba swallowed in a country of ectoplasm; parasites housed in white, in wall; & everything human escapes itself—

call it microbial. call it organism. call
it specimen resembling life in its own
fluid. call it human. anyways. say we
are all one & call it ~~genetic~~ kinship. or
biodiversity. call it learned anaerobic
respiration. call it reverse speciation,
invasive habitat. call it hands
~~un~~wanted. call it colonization by
scalpel. or needle. call it spectacle. call
it sterilization, ~~new face of terrorism~~.
call it ~~white~~ [edit: this isn't about race]
lives saved. call it good of mankind.
call it future of medicine. call it ~~brown~~
[edit: stop making this about race]
sacrifice. call it experimental. call it
~~ethnic~~ cleansing. call it terminal. call
it ceaseless. call it God not prayed to.

***

science says we must be precise about what we call a thing.
when you say *apolitical, my research is apolitical,* do you mean
to say *genocidal?* do you mean to say,
yes, i am a massacre of needles—

~~palestinian/queer~~ specimen attempts to define an algebraic structure for their inherited traumas

Theorem (Seifert–van Kampen): Let X denote the topological space known as the self, as generated by parent spaces U1 and U2. The map, k, defined below, is an injection from the parents onto the trauma the children's body inherits.

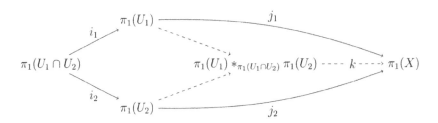

instead of a proof: a translation. since this was all your higher education could not afford you—a language for the dimensionality of the empty you house.

let kernel(j_1) = the arabic you un-inherited, lost in the projection. hence the kernel is trivial, hence the mapping is one-to-one, hence by correspondence you are the image of your parents' assimilations. a gentrification of yourself. the same argument applies for the second parent, kernel(j_2), i.e. the history does in fact repeat itself in the appropriate lineage. a symmetry, of sorts.

the rest of our argument is trivial: the topological properties of space are preserved under these isomorphic mappings. the proof is self-evident, hence goes without saying, much like a translation.

the ~~palestinian/queer~~ specimen's Lexicon with Auto-Translate

once, a language failed me & i hadn't a home
to claim in my own throat—

in Arabic, the word for *tonsil* translates to
daughters of the ears—

we are taught that to have a body is to carry
its lineage inside of us—

& i've tried to make a language where my body
is just my body, my blood just my blood—

but my tongue rejected it. spat it out
like a mouthful of Arabic—

maybe it was defense mechanism; maybe it's the only
way i know how to cough up blood, or History—

***

i was never taught Arabic growing up
    [*translation*—my father never wanted my *throat* to become *threat*]

i don't watch the news anymore
    [*translation*—i am worried my people might be on it]

it is, as they say, tomorrow's history
    [*translation*—hence always written by the victors]

i mean to say, it repeats itself
    [*translation*—i've come to expect the obvious outcome, a learned helplessness]

i saw a girl die on facebook & the video autoplayed
    [*translation*—how do i mourn without a language to name our dead]

& repeated. & repeated. & repeated. &
    [*translation*—i am always translating]

memory study with ~~Elizabeth~~ specimen as lighthouse, in spacetime continuum[1]

or the ghost of my cis gender haunts the genderfluid topology of my body

a lighthouse: there is always: a lighthouse: there is always:
a man: a lighthouse: searching: there is always: hands
searching: the man: the lighthouse: the blood: on his
searching: hands: there is always: a man who claims
he built you: of hands: searching: brief light
-houses: there is always the hands: that made: that
searched: that parted: history: there is always a history:
of hands: trapped: between past: and present: hands
that built: a history: of you: there is always: a you: strong
-blooded: heavy-handed: a lighthouse: an infinity of them:
a trace: a lineage: a man: who claims you: and your non
-linear histories: a man: who searches: an infinity: of dim
-ensions: & impossible: bloodlines: for the work: of his own:
hands: a map: there is always: a map: that leads man: to you:
his own: his blood: searching: a map: a lighthouse: there is always:
a lighthouse: a nail: a door: a man: searching: an infinity: of light
-houses: for you: a map: of history: of men: of him: who built:
an infinity: a bloodline: a you: to conquer: heavy-handed: there is
always: a you: a thing: with blood: and hands: trapped: between two:
impossible: realities: there is always: the man: with an infinity:
of hands: who claims: he built you: always: a you: built: of man:
of hands: this man: these hands: this lighthouse: this search: this want:
this history: these hands: this infinity: in bloodline: searching: reaching:

---

1 **Instructions**: Cut and paste this poem onto a
knotted 3-dimensional realization of a projective
plane—a topological space that cannot exist,
without knotting in on itself at a single point,
in dimensions lower than 4. The "you" is to
be placed at the point of singularity; the paths
stemming from the "you" merely conform to the
topology of the space. This poem is a trajectory
from the self, back to the self.

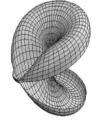

the ~~palestinian/queer~~ specimen's index

the first time a boy craved me,
he said i want what my god

refuses me, his fingers gracing
my young lips; we were home

alone & the blood wanted what
it could not conjure; i wanted

him, all fist & rapture; i hadn't
a language where affirmation wasn't

a form of self-sabotage; i let
boyhood answer his call & my breath

was not my breath; my lips,
the captives begging a collapsing

tomb of his, thick, & ungodly
the refuse which parts atria; he still

called me *fucking queer* & i have since
known queer to mean desire

my god refused me. or
forsaken. blood of lamb.

think sacrilege, crucifixion by mouth,
much like *luti*, translated people

of Lot; sinners of Sodom; maybe if i
meant *no*, i wouldn't be sin

& exile in every language that claims
me; i want لا to lack desire's tangibility

unlike نعم which, birthed heavy
in the lungs, can corrode breath,

hence *un*voice; in this language
i want to make every *no* as inescapable

as the voice it clings to; a gentle
لا can kiss the tongue & close

23

a throat in the same breath & i
wonder if that too is a self

-colonization; to un-mother the mouth,
strip the altar of its sacrifice; let this

body be, instead, a lighthouse;
let me converge at the point

where all wanderers intersect
unbloodied, even in want; if desire is,

as my language translates, *a moon,*
let this body be the satellite

who learned its own escape velocity;
let our bodies be not endings,

but the journeys themselves—
let my words, instead of endless litany,

be an index, unhinging the foundations
of every category & name forced upon

us & let that be biblical. watch us
rewrite graves into sunrise—ceaseless

fractal—call us scripters
of breath, for every silence that failed

us; every trachea collapsing
under its own weight—

maqam of moonlight, for the wandering
to be read from right to left, after Marwa Helal

a ask to—   blood of conjuring a is desire of know i what
&   sweat its in humid   listless it was or   me of nation tired
—deviance quantum &   stochasticity own its in   lost   : entropy
carries it   blood the hence &   design its through thing a name to learned we
type what—is it night of type what on depending   to or—on preys &
carries   air the humid   heavy of

relics fragile   before   you like   men ruined i've yes
count body my   marked i   catacomb brief a chest   themselves of
lose   never beast this lest   erosion refusing   scar it let &   nails brittle with
made he caverns the   forget or marrow of   dry sucked   bones of count
endless &   unexplored   perimeters its in even yes : flight   refusing skeletons of
planet   this heart   sweet   reach   beyond stratosphere or   body as
—us of both the for   claustrophobic   too is

on unraveling

i never wanted   to unlove you
like this: trees   shivering thread-
bare in fracturing   chill; faint body
shadows   dancing   behind subway
lights like   drifting   ghosts;
the city undressing   itself
of you   like a music   -less season—
        i have never known   winter this
intimately.   Here's the street   we waltzed
in huddled   coats, our breaths,   intertwining
smoke   vortices, i only wanted   someone
to inhale   the substance   of me—to make
Atlas of   your hands & tear down   my sky in
slow motion;   snowflakes   pirouetting, chaotic
axes—i loved best the flurry   of you. Every time
i'd empty myself   of your memory, the distance
frostbit   my lungs & i   would make sanctuary
of your bed,   becoming constricting   throat &
tachycardia   again—here's the   train station
you first abandoned   me to meet her, like you
didn't hear   glass screaming   on your way
out; here's   the window   i almost embraced
too lovingly   & became   the snow   -fall;
here's   the street i first   imploded on you for
the devil   you fell in   love with   & i get
it—we all   have to   dance with   demons
to find   God in   ourselves   & maybe that's
the only   way i know   how to love—   to give my
        self, blessed   sacrifice, to a   God of
        unraveling hands;   most holy   inconvenience,
i found home   in your type   of empty. By which
i mean,   i found myself   in you & i know you
intended   none of this; God   of scalding fingers
& emerging   firestorm; you,   who resurrected
me from   my own tomb,   gauze wrapped & blood
-stained, i know   you didn't mean   to kill me. You
were two years of   trauma & arms   i could die in;
there's praise   in being held so   tightly i almost felt
human again. In warmth   expelling winter's loneliness
from my architecture.   In the infinitesimal
fragment of you   that lives   & swells in me; it
sings to me   some nights.   A lullaby that
could numb   a warfront quiet;   there's resistance in
that. This pulsing   riot. Maybe i loved best the

rebellion of us;   two diasporas folding
into each other   in a single bed frame, ashes
to ashes, dust to   dust; still here
we're still   breathing—

~~palestinian/queer~~ specimen attempts to define an algebraic structure for their inherited traumas

Theorem (Mayer-Vietoris Sequence): Let X denote the body as a topological space. Let A denote the depression, and B the queerness. Let A ∩ B denote the intersection of the two. For any space, S, let $H_k(S)$ denote the kth homology group of that space—a topological invariant representing the nature of k-dimensional holes in that space. The following sequence is exact in all dimensions:

$$\cdots \to H_{n+1}(X) \xrightarrow{\partial_*} H_n(A \cap B) \xrightarrow{(i_*, j_*)} H_n(A) \oplus H_n(B) \xrightarrow{k_* - l_*} H_n(X) \xrightarrow{\partial_*}$$
$$\xrightarrow{\partial_*} H_{n-1}(A \cap B) \to \cdots \to H_0(A) \oplus H_0(B) \xrightarrow{k_* - l_*} H_0(X) \to 0.$$

instead of a proof: a history. if X is the self, covered by spaces A and B, haunted in some topological sense, then we begin with generation n+1. Via the injective mapping of ∂_*, your aunt (generation n) inherited the shape of her emptiness from the boundaries of her mother's trauma. an ocean, projected onto a whole ancestry, projected into the intersection of your aunt's queerness & depression, denoted $H_n(A \cap B)$. & before she was a pale, blue thing rotting in the vomit of her own overdose, she was the queer body, splayed & split from itself. hence, the injections (i_*, j_*) denoted a time her depression & queerness were two (2) distinct entities, a separation, $H_n(A) \oplus H_n(B)$, destined to converge into a single body. Hence, the map $k_* - l_*$ is a map, from the product space of your queer & your mind, into the haunted body. the time her mother said *you just need help, a therapist, a nice woman to excise this demon from you*, is proof enough of this haunting & separation from self. a projection of a mother's trauma (i.e. abuse, i.e. alcoholism, i.e. expulsion) means your aunt's wholeness was defined by her queerness & depression, hence her own emptiness.

& at this point, it may be appropriate to ask where your body fits into the picture: at the boundary of your aunt's trauma? at the infinite intersection of all that came before you? are you to be crafted in your aunt's image, then splayed, then split, projection child of her anxieties?

the algorithm goes: parent loses a country only to beg a country of their children. children build their own country, or lose themselves in the process. the sequence terminates. in the case that the children do not lose themselves, they pass on the weight of their ghost countries to their children, who themselves lose this country & another. & another. the induction is self-evident.

memory study, in fragmented reality

in this reality, i am a boy
who kisses his lover beneath
the fireworks—july 4, 2012.
the last girl i wore on my breath
apologizes before calling me
faggot, an observation.
& perhaps this copy of myself
even replied *thank you* & wasn't
a ghost sifting in the floorboards
of its own home; in another
body, this is the story
-book ending: the ending
where even i come out
                  alive—

                  *

i want to say i love my mother
like the four-year copy of myself:
my chubby hand open & waving,
catching air, sticky with saliva
& sweet crystalline residue;
how even in infancy i craved most
that which could end or define
me, an unknowing symmetry;
a red serum dissolving & trickling
down my cheek like Styx—

                  *

Thales hypothesized that all matter was
composed of water droplets.
i'd like to think there exists a world
where everything i touch becomes
both desire & inheritance; permutations
of a former self; hence, i could absolve
myself this body; & every time
a lover entered me, they could taste
a country on fire: the freedom
to deform,
                  & forget—

                  *

in this reality, my mother's liver was,
instead, a drawbridge; her hands were not
minotaurs escaping a burning kingdom,
my brother was not her child forsaken
& crucified; we did not have to beg a
half-sung religion from her ocean-liner
vertebrae, as if they were not the aftermath
of partitioned countries; my mother was not
southern transplant, or daughter
of floodwater; instead, the mountain
forgave the river its dry
-drowning; instead, the bloodied ethanol
climbed up the cliffs of her throat—

                    *

say the marrow forgave its captor, bone—
& even that is its own form of shelter;
say a bruise is just a rebellion of blood,
a rupture of capillaries & all the ghosts they
failed to contain & is that not the body
in its primal beauty? what of the self
can evolve without breakage
            of touch?

                    *

my mother, in her purest anger, reminds me
of a reality where she birthed me drugless:
the expense   of me,   the splitting
of her,   of atom, of umbilical cord stretching
oceans; isn't the mother   in exile an act of self
-dispossession? i am both   child & ransacked
temple in Her   image, hence   premonition
of flesh, in all its brief   partings; of a lineage
which craves most   its own
            collapse—

                    *

what of the body isn't
an unbecoming—

                    *

in this reality, the story unwrites itself:
my lover un-ghosts me after i swallow

confession; the word *bisexual* unmakes
itself at home in me & i do not leave
my house; the clear liquid runs back
into its bottle like a river might; my mother
is not yet a mountain: the avalanche sweeps
up her body, unlearning & inhaling its anxieties;
she's a good girl, a good southern girl:
the future grandchildren of my mother's sentences
retreat to a hypothetical womb; her blessing, not
formed, hangs heavy in the thick air; my queerness
& self-loathing unwind, like DNA strands—

*

today a white doctor who is, perhaps,
a surgeon, draws a river of knotted blood;
is it in your family history? a red punctuation
mark swelling on my forearm & today i am
my father's stubborn child; *there's nothing
a bit of exercise won't fix*; even blood?
i wonder but do not ask; *tell me about this
history of anxiety* & i want to say it is
my blood; my veins, the churches crowded
in the aftermath & is that not desire?
to crave most a coping which un-empties
the body; i inhale my gut & it is no less
a knotted anchor; i am no less stranger
in these waters; i call it *southern
hospitality*; i practice good manners:
i am teaching myself the slowest way
to disappear—

*

i uncork a bottle of liquid galaxies
& tonight i am my mother's child;
a boy i find pretty presses his tongue
against my front teeth & i forget
myself;   i later find
my self   alone beneath
the star   light & this
is not   the reality where
the boy loves himself back, nor is it
a story where the boy needn't hate
himself to be worthy of touch—

*

say the sweet tooth bites back. carnal:
say he didn't make me swallow   his country
& its brief sunrise that night & i cannot say this
is this not what i wanted—to crave most what seeks
to end itself inside of me? what of the self
can evolve without fracture? without man
entering its kingdom, all floodgate & storybook
& tonight i am not my mother's child, but a boy
convincing a copy of himself that this is the ending
desire gifted him: the boy, kissing a parallel copy
of his lover beneath fireworks—in any case, the story
ends in implosion; in any case, the boy is both fuse
        & detonation—

*

tonight i am a thousand miles north
& i do not call my mother. i do not
smell the ethanol through her phone
-static; i do not hear the same apology
unwinding itself from her breath
like collapsing rosary beads; like *allah*
yerhama whispered at a wake; but i do
hear her say *i love you, you have to know*
i love you. & is that not its own funeral
quiet? her hands, kissing the bottle's rim
        submerging in the absence—

*

say the sun forgave itself the inevitable
disappearance; say the ocean forgave
the moonlight's lonesome pull—
say the fluid forgave its captor,
        history—
& even that can be its own shelter;
maybe in that reality, i would be,
instead, child of Thales: descendant
of salt & molecule; everything i touch,
spiraling into a galaxy of droplets,
        dissolving—

maqam of moonlight, for the children of exile
to be read from right to left, after Marwa Helal

silver-lunged of wealth dying on talk the me Spare
clean—goodbye thread last His kissed i .Gods
sky the taste almost could i—woundless sliver
Love everything—tongue on pearl—Him of empty
rain i : intractable love i : yes—me afford couldn't
language a haven't i—arabic brittle a speak i : cobalt
swallow only can world the—daylight in   digestible
: say i so & me of   impermanence brash the
—himself of death[1] the write boy-thing the let
—carnivore its choose & summon prey the let
a of less any he is man another for dies he if
?behind leaves he myths the than revolution
before died who those than beast a less any he is
?waving & draped keffiyeh—fisted clenched—him

---

1 تَسْتَقِلَّ أَنْ هَمُّهُ يَكِلَّ لَنْ الشبابُ
يَبِيدْ أو يَبِيدْ أو

memory study with ~~Elizabeth~~ specimen as apocalypse

what you know of   history is a conjuring   of endless winter; in this
reality, a decade   of torture, cast upon your   body makes you body
of bloodied riot,   memory   jaded

     waning under the dust
     of you—of men & their science
     who built a dictator   in you & the universe, you
     inherited—who built
     Atlas of you—

     placed the weight of their
     world on your shoulders
     & begged an un-collapsing

genesis; in this reality, you are
a god in some sense. Galaxies

     unravel under the rage
     of you, a drunk architecture
of limbs, horizons swept
into a singularity & all the stars

     on your breath: the weapon
     they made of your infinity—

     in the wrong hands,
     you are body of endless

     rapture; the beautiful
     devastation of endless

     histories repeating them
     -selves, of endless

     fruition, a lineage
     of hands, of endless

     wreckage, of
     body   endless—

     of endless

     of endless

     of endless

[counter/terrorism]

the history goes, the first Intifada   was a rain   of teeth.
Shin Bet marveled   at the beast   they created & became   a celebration
of bullets. this mid-east   Frankenstein. this brown   rebirth. fangs bare.
& dripping.

i once found home   in the empty between   clenched jawlines.
& that was the street my mother   grew up where *sand   n███* flew out of
the mouth   of a stranger,   who was *settler*   in this country.
that's not   the point. i mean,   what does an immigrant call it
when   they have no home   to go back to?

once, i wrote down   history & it was not   a lie,
by which i mean   my hands were not   dripping,
i did not create   a massacre in the   erasure
& a white woman called me *crazy   he's just crazy* & i
became body   of gritted teeth. of   rising smoke,
exhaust from the torched city of me.

>   *are you beside yourself yet? / have you retreated to your white god*
>   *-forsaken sanctuary? / am i* **SECURITY THREAT** */ enough?*

the history goes, israeli   settler expansion was illegal   under international law.
until it wasn't. that's not   the point. the settlers were fleeing   *religious*
persecution, much like pilgrim   settlers fled for America. i mean,
what is colonization   if not an aftermath   of hands,
of men   searching for home?

& i am the wrong landmass   to beg a home   of. just barely
a floating   body. stone   who refused to dance   on water:
the oppressor knows not   your howl, the way you   splice
the air   & that   is freedom song.

video footage: israeli soldier   shoots child   armed   with
stone.   point blank.   minutes later, his cousin   exile
with the sun in her hair   punches the soldier   square
in the face—   takes history   into her own   hands—

i still don't know what to do with my hands in history class.

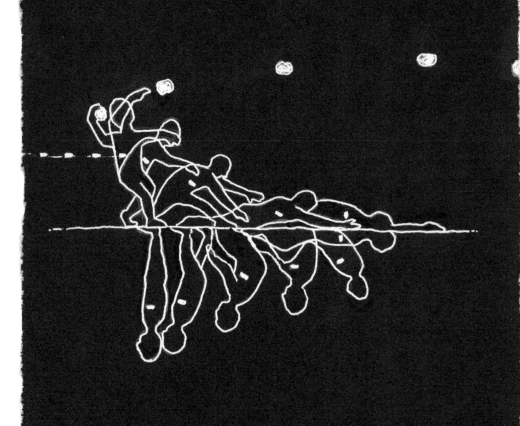

ars poetica in which every pronoun is a Free Palestine

& so it is written: the settlers will steal God's land & FREE PALESTINE
will curse the settlers with an inability to season FREE PALESTINE's food,

a sunburn the shape of the settler dictator's face on every body untanned
who will claim FREE PALESTINE's earth but not FREE PALESTINE's skin

soil-stained. there. FREE PALESTINE said it. no one really owns anything FREE
PALESTINE didn't unwrite to make it so—FREE PALESTINE's sea

israeli; FREE PALESTINE's sky *israeli* but not FREE PALESTINE's thunder—
the blame will always be FREE PALESTINE's & so this will be called an accurate

history; the expense of FREE PALESTINE's visibility, willed in bloodied cloth—
or paper—FREE PALESTINE's longest suicide: FREE PALESTINE will die

in jail & become *israeli*—FREE PALESTINE will die in protest & become
kite on fire— FREE PALESTINE will call Hamas fable of every

HEADLINE: israeli falafel so dry FREE PALESTINE could start an intifada with it—
HEADLINE: israeli falafel so dry FREE PALESTINE could free Palestine with it—

no, FREE PALESTINE will never give FREE PALESTINE's self a name
not rooted in upheaval—FREE PALESTINE, hyphenated by settler flag:

FREE PALESTINE hyphenated by settler pronouns: FREE PALESTINE will not
pledge allegiance to Arabic. or English. FREE PALESTINE will exist

in no language—FREE PALESTINE will write poems of olive tree & checkpoint
& no Free Palestine to be found—FREE PALESTINE will name the violence

& never the resurrection, like FREE PALESTINE hasn't survived impossible
histories to get here—it is written: the blood will be on FREE PALESTINE's hands

might as well paint FREE PALESTINE's nails while FREE PALESTINE's
at it—what? is this not what FREE PALESTINE expected? did FREE PALESTINE

not think FREE PALESTINE would have the last laugh all along?

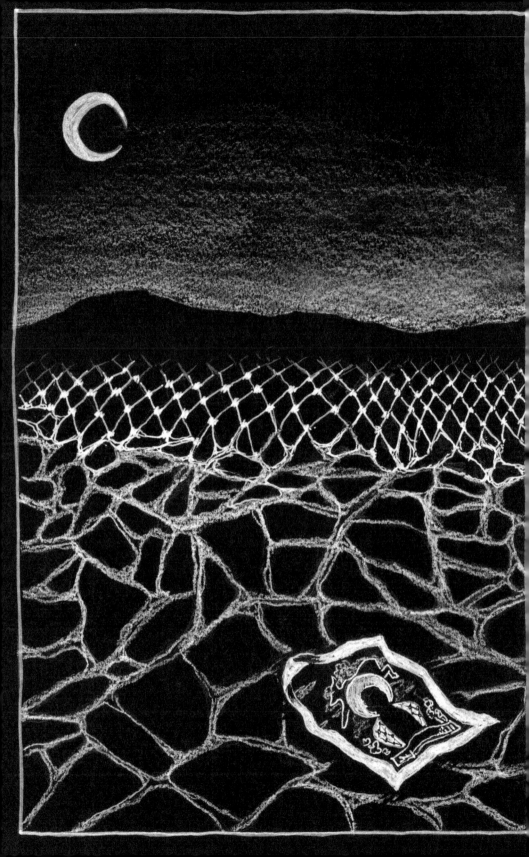

maqam of moonlight, for the children of exile

to be read from right to left, after Marwa Helal

—keffiyeh a wear to ways of hundreds are there
chest your let—flag like neck your across it drape
hung of ornamentation the—it of sharp the absorb
love in country a is too that maybe &—bodies
perpendicular geometry a—borders jagged its with
upon died Gods your cross the or teeth exposed as
needle-stitched & rebellion tiny of cloth—graceless
—bodied until : bloodied[1] until bloodless : skin
type right the in you become it let : it behind hide
make it seen i've : you strangle it let : dark of
—gaze my beneath beasts tamest the of martyrs
: aesthetic stone : glitterbomb radar : scatter limb

?lovers country's invisible an of fate the this is
?empty night's to yourself gifting not if love is what

---

1 للعِدَى نكونّ ولنْ الرّدَى منَ نَستقي

43

the ~~palestinian/queer~~ specimen's apology

it is the summer   after my spleen almost ruptured   into the stain
of a thousand sunsets.   i am in a therapist's office.   she asks me to start at
the moment i wanted to die   from my own hands.

      i could have painted her this   body, in all its failed topologies;

(i haven't a home ~~that isn't in love with the way it floods~~

but instead, i gave her a history lesson:

,nakba after   israel by annexed bank west—1967
;home own their in   exiled grandparents my

(when i say, anxiety stretches   ~~continents;~~
(when i say, depression is an ocean   ~~we never wanted~~
                ~~to traverse—~~

      fast forward—

my aunt falls
      in love with
            a woman twice
                  her age; finds
         mother in her
after her own grieved
      a stolen country,
             husband with blood
      full of fists;
(when she comes out, they ask if she needs to see a therapist—

               —her in devil the excise to woman nice a

      fast forward to today—

a stranger | with fists | in his | blood | makes a growing country | of my organs

(& i cannot love ~~myself—~~

or perhaps, this is just a lesson in topology—a professor who fails me tells the class of exact
sequences; how topological spaces inherit the shape of their emptiness from previous generations
of dimensions; a whole lineage of singularities, and at this point, i too wanted to disappear,
in the office of this therapist, who was, perhaps, a topologist, who asks,

               ?you of inside take anxiety this does shape what so

& i wanted to say tooth   of a mouth, eye of a hurricane   in my chest, an organ
                                          with vast chambers   haunted by its own
                                                                                    emptiness
                                                                              & so much blood,

(it can almost be mistaken for a country
/ newfound inheritance
/ atheism found at the intersection of 3 merciless gods—

                              ?praying stopped you have why ?still pray you do
the therapist asks
& perhaps the therapist is
my mother; the one who found god
at the bottom of liquor bottles the color of blood
-ied oceans; the hands that prayed for a son who left
in search for home; desire, swelling in him like a ruptured organ;

                                        father, forgive me my drunk inheritance—

                                                            forgive the stairs that
                                                            collapsed   beneath
                                                            the weight of me
                                                            : forgive the third
                                                            floor window that
                                                            tried   to   swallow
                                                            me into the night's
                                                            mouth : forgive the
                                                            bodies i swallowed
                                                            like broken teeth,
                                                            the knees i spent
                                                            trying to summon
                                                            god in my own
                                                            mouth : forgive my
                                                            DNA   strands, for
                                                            they are sculptors of
                                                            brief suicides in this
                                                            body—

i'm trying to love
the shattered window
of myself—
                        the hands,
                                                      the rocks,
                        the broken religion
                        left behind—

(my inheritance is a body of vandalized cathedrals—

light me on fire;
                        strip my god
                        from my breath;
                                                      watch as i dance
                                                      amidst the flames—

45

memory study
with ~~Elizabeth~~ specimen
at baptism

you killed a man today.
let his blood darken
the waters he found
himself in; found his
god in; before he birthed
one; yes, the infinity
the history, the dim
-ensions placed on you
makes you god, child;
which makes you bloody
-handed, yes, but at his
expense, you escaped
the massacre of your
-self; made all the
necessary wounds to get
here, with your God,
his lungs emptying
beneath the surface
of his own making;
Father, isn't this everything
you asked of your greatest
creations? to quiet
the pulse of every blood
seeking to end you?
what of the self can exist
after it destroys its maker?
isn't this the most graceless
suicide; to escape not only
the body, but the history
it was born into—

Essay on Submission

Having ebbed in the disbelief of it instead of its weight.

Stone-tiled the floor the blood a trickling fire confessional.

Here the ocean metaphor refused.

He tore me shut & seeping no vastness.

To marvel or hide in.

Being told i don't exist i laugh with wounded teeth into.

The folds of his larynx a choir of bees rattle me.

Into myth less the mechanics of.

Throat than the usage the context neither divorced from combustion.

Of birth more or less i forgave him before.

He entered because he swelled for me i could never trust.

Myself in his hands but i did want.

Him.

Knocking leaning into the sliver of light a peeled condom.

Missed the wastebasket he couldn't bear.

The sight of me i never slept.

With the lights off i don't know that.

History.

But i named it so it can't be.

Holy.

Or rather question.

Of distance my skin.

And cold waters my skin and woundless.

Skin i wade in the contradiction.

After i wanted only to be.

Held.

No.

Distance his hand & the small of my.

Back his hand & the lip.

Of a waterfall here i reject the landscape.

Its vastness i don't think.

We're looking for the same thing you.

And I you'd think olympus.

Would dethrone itself of goldenrod leaves i told you it was.

Blood did i claim it.

Mine i am built of avoidable.

Violences with one drop apocalypse.

The burning wilderness you can see yourself.

Out now histories like this cannot.

Be known let alone escaped even the one.

Where i set fire to my colonizer i can afford neither.

Reclamation nor reconciliation.

No.

Unfragmented i cannot give you an ending.

That isn't body lunar.

And concave staining instead.

The bathroom floor.

ars poetica with parallel dimensions

i must confess, this softness is often an endless
well
      i fall into, the way a snake chases itself into
itself. on tamer days
              i blame the fruit for their thick
ripening & not the small jealousies
                      endangering
the honeybee; some days i cannot distinguish
desire
      & extinction—every love of mine demands blood
-shed of a hunter
          's lineage; o exile my exile, that i could
unbloody our laced talons
        & write them into metal
wings; that we could un-cauterize the crimson
           sky & fly
into a sunset spilling blood that is not our own—
the love that turns
       2 mirrors in on themselves,
unraveling those infinite & countable dimensions;
  somewhere, i pluck an apple   & a parallel self suffers
   the expulsion, itself   ancestry rippling across space, itself
    timeless; in this reality, i lose   a country,
      for another Eden   to blossom beneath
      a more forgiving stratosphere;
      i confess, i am more vengeful than my oppressors
      deem me; my disposition
              is a learned
          burial—
i fang so hard it louds my smile, writes my cyanide
ducts into gentle
        rain; in truth, i wish them an
        eternity
of carnage for every country they stole
          from us,
the way infinity plus infinity is just infinity;
forever fails us
      like that; our eternity is the moment
between child's fist
      & soldier's gun; i know threat
is not object but state
        (of being); because i
     love him,
he is everyone's
      threat; i bloody my hands for
  him,

so he must be God
             of somewhere; i know heaven
is a poem i survive
                      the end of; i know
            holy
is waking up
             with a knotted neck
                          on a crowded
red sofa in Philadelphia; i know that
                         is a country
             even i can have
                      faith in—

"There is no loneliness when you have the whole world inside of you."

– Vanessa Meng

Post-Script: Against Consolidation

i want to write about the blueberries i picked from the throat of a New England fall afternoon; how my hands plucked each branch like a familiar melody.

& suddenly, it is 2008. i am small and unremarkable, standing in a blueberry orchard in northern california with my brown cousins. maybe summer is a form of muscle memory.

it is important to mention that the word brown in the previous sentence was used unironically, so as to normalize the existence of a particular subject in a particular landscape. one could call this poem a form of painting, but that would assume it exists within a physical color scheme & landscape, neither of which are essential to the poem's existence.

i mean to say, this is a poem about muscle memory—a phenomenon which, after decades of studies, still has no explanation. a leading theory suggests that memories undergo consolidation: the process of stabilization from short- to long-term memory.

perhaps we can infer the existence of a thing without knowing its internal structure; perhaps, like music, the hands remember even when the ear cannot; the body remembers a music by the hollow dancing it leaves behind—

many mathematical proofs of existence rely on inference & the limitations of a given logical framework, as opposed to an explicit construction. hence, we can construct sets for which we can assign no logical measure without being able to visualize or even describe them abstractly.

one tool for such proofs of existence is the axiom of choice—metaphorically speaking, it too is a form of unconscious memory. it states that, given a tree with infinite branches, it is possible to pluck one blueberry from each branch—

that's not the point. i mean, choice is not inherent to every system of logic.

the first time i learned *choice is not inherent to every system of logic* was not in the context of mathematics, or countries,   or bodies.

i want to write about my country & mean *country*. such a silly tithe, forgiving sacrifice; something i didn't have to cough out like praying with tiny flags caught in my teeth.

i want to write a poem about home & not have to mean country. or death—or how easily the two can be mistaken for one another—

one could say this is a consequence of neither concept being well-defined; hence the lack of a former can give rise to a definitive latter, or vice versa, in most logical frameworks.

a professor warns me that a consequence of the axiom of choice leads to many mathematical paradoxes that violate our conceptions of mass, space, and time. such ill-desired behavior is labelled *pathological*.

for instance, it is possible to decompose one sphere into two identical spheres, hence four hence infinitely many; from one life, springs two, hence four, hence infinitely many.

one could say death is poorly defined in such a logical framework.

or perhaps every death is an unobservable construction; consider, for instance, the ancestors resurrected in every poem. how i was fluent in the language of their death before ever being fluent in the Arabic they spoke before me—*allah yerhama, allah yerhama*—

& perhaps this is the job of the poet, much like the mathematician; to give language to that which cannot be constructed; to un-eviscerate the flesh, give muscle memory to every chaos of limbs.

1998—my earliest memory is being lost in a sea of cousins at a Christmas party. i do not stand out from the crowd until the dabke starts—the music shaking the floor beneath my tiny feet & i dance like there is no earthquake beneath me; so i dance & part my cousins like every ocean my ancestors split before me; like my body knew i was Palestinian before i did—

or maybe it was the lurch of my gut the last time i visited my queer aunt's unmarked grave; how even in remembrance, her ghost was but an erasure of her former self.

it is important to mention that the last woman i loved was buried in the same cemetery, just yards away, & yet, i have spanned entire galaxies & failed poems trying to reconstruct her laughter; how the body remembers not the beloved but the music she left behind—

how the last time i visited her grave, the gray skies parted, no metaphor, leaking light onto blank stone for the first time all week & in coincidence or faith, i am inclined to call that grace—

i want to write about tiny miracles: i woke up this morning. i woke up this morning.

contrary to expectation, the repetition in the previous statement was not intended to provide emphasis, and yet, you are inclined to revisit the sentiment once more. one could say this is an instance of *pathological* behavior.

or perhaps the first noted instance of pathological behavior was when i first mentioned the word *country*. or the space between countries & bodies in line 9.

perhaps, since this is a poem about memory, it is discontinuous by necessity; there are hands, hence there will always be breakage—

current neurological theory argues against consolidation; says that, perhaps, memories never stabilize, but are encoded in parallel architectures.

this suggests we encode reality in multiplicities, hence, every perception of reality is, by construction, a multiverse of complexity.

i want to write about the first Arab i met in grad school like she wasn't a miracle; or maybe every Palestinian is a parallel universe.

i want to write about new year's eve in Bethlehem: the house, swelling with cousins & their pillowfight laughter. i want to talk about george, who was always first to throw the pillow but had the sweetest face when his mother came around; his father outside, roasting kabab, talking about those fuckers & their checkpoints ruining his morning commute; & nathalie who paraded her hand-stitched gowns throughout the house like she owned the place & in the same breath, lectured us on god's grace; how jesus cured her cancer before the chemo could; she sounded so much like my teta i swear i was home or at least somewhere she was allowed to exist whole; i want to write about nadia who knew more english than her mother & still counted down to midnight in arabic; the whole house, dancing to a music they didn't know but understood; i want to remember my homeland this way: the city alight but not ablaze.

i want to write about nights in Palestine where the last thing we thought about was death; about being smoked out in Ramallah like she knows she'll rise with barbed wire teeth & a steel-tipped boot to the face; that reality exists without saying, so give us tonight to dance without words—

let me remember, first, the dance & not the ensuing exile; let me write about home without writing its unbecoming—

& i confess, i have spent too much time revolving around my own unbecoming; the way time dilates around a black hole, reality diverging at the point where not even light escapes—

i confess, dear reader, that by reading this you have become my new test subject: the specimen is biting back. i speak not of this poem, but of the memory of it—the parallel worlds your mind will inhabit, patching together my every image in your universe of perception.

i mean to say, there will always be a universe in your mind & in that universe, there will always be a Palestine with children laughing.

men have turned entire countries into test subjects without their consent. neither the men nor countries are named in this poem, so as to restrict this reality from the universes of this poem.

& it follows that every poem is a false god; maybe not in sin but in the confession of it all: how every implosion is only beautiful in unraveling—not in the breath held before the collapse

between poem   & reality   & perception of poem
     in the fringes   between reality & perception of reality—
i began this poem   THE SYSTEM DOES NOT CONVERGE with blueberries
with muscle memory   THE SYSTEM DOES NOT CONVERGE   & hands—
                 (or maybe i never had control
                  over the narrative—)
being ill-defined   THE SYSTEM DOES NOT CONVERGE   when i say
               THE SYSTEM DOES NOT CONVERGE   His hands
               THE SYSTEM DOES NOT CONVERGE   smelled like
               THE SYSTEM DOES NOT CONVERGE   blueberries, I mean
California, 2008,   THE SYSTEM DOES NOT CONVERGE
i am small & insignificant   THE SYSTEM   Philadelphia, 2015:
            (yes, He made a massacre of me—
            (yes, i was his   for the taking—
               DOES NOT   i am small
               CONVERGE   i am insignificant
the poem is circling back   THE SYSTEM DOES NOT   & diverging
the poem assumes multiple   CONVERGE   realities,
meanings   THE SYSTEM DOES NOT CONVERGE   the hands
in this way   THE SYSTEM FAILS   the poem intersects
                 TO CONVERGE   with the reality of
            THE SYSTEM DOES NOT CONVERGE   the reader
the poem remembers   THE SYSTEM DOES NOT CONVERGE   what the
            THE SYSTEM DOES NOT CONVERGE   reader cannot
the hands,   THE SYSTEM DOES NOT CONVERGE   always—
            (the hands, for instance
            the poem remembers always   the hands—
           THE SYSTEM DOES NOT CONVERGE
           THE SYSTEM DOES NOT CONVERGE
           THE POEM DOES NOT CONVERGE
           THE POEM FAILS TO CONVERGE
           THE SYSTEM DOES NOT CONVERGE
           THE SYSTEM FAILS TO CONVERGE

THE SYSTEM FAILS TO CONVERGE
THE SYSTEM FAILS TO CONVERGE THE SYSTEM FAILS TO CONVERGE
THE SYSTEM FAILS TO CONVERGE THE SYSTEM FAILS TO CONVERGE
THE SYSTEM FAILS TO CONVERGE
THE SYSTEM FAILS TO CONVERGE THE SYSTEM FAILS TO CONVERGE
THE SYSTEM FAILS TO CONVERGE
THE SYSTEM FAILS TO CONVERGE THE SYSTEM FAILS TO CONVERGE
THE SYSTEM FAILS TO CONVERGE
THE SYSTEM FAILS TO CONVERGE THE SYSTEM FAILS TO CONVERGE
THE SYSTEM FAILS TO CONVERGE
THE SYSTEM FAILS TO CONVERGE THE SYSTEM FAILS TO CONVERGE
THE SYSTEM FAILS TO CONVERGE
THE SYSTEM FAILS TO CONVERGE THE SYSTEM FAILS TO CONVERGE
THE SYSTEM FAILS TO CONVERGE
THE SYSTEM FAILS TO CONVERGE THE SYSTEM FAILS TO CONVERGE
THE SYSTEM FAILS TO CONVERGE
THE SYSTEM FAILS TO CONVERGE THE SYSTEM FAILS TO CONVERGE
THE SYSTEM FAILS TO CONVERGE
THE SYSTEM FAILS TO CONVERGE THE SYSTEM FAILS TO CONVERGE
THE SYSTEM FAILS TO CONVERGE
THE SYSTEM FAILS TO CONVERGE THE SYSTEM FAILS TO CONVERGE
THE SYSTEM FAILS TO CONVERGE
THE SYSTEM FAILS TO CONVERGE THE SYSTEM FAILS TO CONVERGE
THE SYSTEM FAILS TO CONVERGE
THE SYSTEM FAILS TO CONVERGE THE SYSTEM FAILS TO CONVERGE
THE SYSTEM FAILS TO CONVERGE
THE SYSTEM FAILS TO CONVERGE THE SYSTEM FAILS TO CONVERGE
THE SYSTEM FAILS TO CONVERGE
THE SYSTEM FAILS TO CONVERGE THE SYSTEM FAILS TO CONVERGE
THE SYSTEM FAILS TO CONVERGE
THE SYSTEM FAILS TO CONVERGE THE SYSTEM FAILS TO CONVERGE
THE SYSTEM FAILS TO CONVERGE
THE SYSTEM FAILS TO CONVERGE THE SYSTEM FAILS TO CONVERGE
THE SYSTEM FAILS TO CONVERGE
THE SYSTEM FAILS TO CONVERGE THE SYSTEM FAILS TO CONVERGE
THE SYSTEM FAILS TO CONVERGE
THE SYSTEM FAILS TO CONVERGE THE SYSTEM FAILS TO CONVERGE
THE SYSTEM FAILS TO CONVERGE
THE SYSTEM FAILS TO CONVERGE THE SYSTEM FAILS TO CONVERGE
THE SYSTEM FAILS TO CONVERGE
THE SYSTEM FAILS TO CONVERGE THE SYSTEM FAILS TO CONVERGE
THE SYSTEM FAILS TO CONVERGE
THE SYSTEM FAILS TO CONVERGE THE SYSTEM FAILS TO CONVERGE
THE SYSTEM FAILS TO CONVERGE
THE SYSTEM FAILS TO CONVERGE THE SYSTEM FAILS TO CONVERGE
THE SYSTEM FAILS TO CONVERGE
THE SYSTEM FAILS TO CONVERGE THE SYSTEM FAILS TO CONVERGE
THE SYSTEM FAILS TO CONVERGE
THE SYSTEM FAILS TO CONVERGE THE SYSTEM FAILS TO CONVERGE
THE SYSTEM FAILS TO CONVERGE
THE SYSTEM FAILS TO CONVERGE THE SYSTEM FAILS TO CONVERGE
THE SYSTEM FAILS TO CONVERGE
CONVERGE THE SYSTEM FAILS TO CONVERGE
CONVERGE THE SYSTEM FAILS TO CONVERGE
THE SYSTEM FAILS TO CONVERGE THE SYSTEM FAILS TO
CONVERGE THE SYSTEM FAILS TO CONVERGE
CONVERGE THE SYSTEM FAILS TO CONVERGE
THE SYSTEM FAILS TO CONVERGE THE SYSTEM FAILS TO

THE SYSTEM FAILS TO CONVERGE

CONVERGE THE SYSTEM FAILS TO CONVERGE

THE SYSTEM FAILS TO CONVERGE THE SYSTEM FAILS TO

CONVERGE THE SYSTEM FAILS TO CONVERGE

THE SYSTEM FAILS TO CONVERGE THE SYSTEM FAILS TO

CONVERGE THE SYSTEM FAILS TO CONVERGE

THE SYSTEM FAILS TO CONVERGE THE SYSTEM FAILS TO

CONVERGE THE SYSTEM FAILS TO CONVERGE

THE SYSTEM FAILS TO CONVERGE THE SYSTEM FAILS TO

CONVERGE THE SYSTEM FAILS TO CONVERGE

THE SYSTEM FAILS TO CONVERGE THE SYSTEM FAILS TO

CONVERGE THE SYSTEM FAILS TO CONVERGE

THE SYSTEM FAILS TO CONVERGE THE SYSTEM FAILS TO

CONVERGE THE SYSTEM FAILS TO CONVERGE

THE SYSTEM FAILS TO CONVERGE THE SYSTEM FAILS TO

CONVERGE THE SYSTEM FAILS TO CONVERGE

THE SYSTEM FAILS TO CONVERGE THE SYSTEM FAILS TO

CONVERGE THE SYSTEM FAILS TO CONVERGE

THE SYSTEM FAILS TO CONVERGE THE SYSTEM FAILS TO

CONVERGE THE SYSTEM FAILS TO CONVERGE

THE SYSTEM FAILS TO CONVERGE THE SYSTEM FAILS TO

CONVERGE THE SYSTEM FAILS TO CONVERGE

THE SYSTEM FAILS TO CONVERGE THE SYSTEM FAILS TO

CONVERGE THE SYSTEM FAILS TO CONVERGE

THE SYSTEM FAILS TO CONVERGE THE SYSTEM FAILS TO

CONVERGE THE SYSTEM FAILS TO CONVERGE

THE SYSTEM FAILS TO CONVERGE THE SYSTEM FAILS TO

CONVERGE THE SYSTEM FAILS TO CONVERGE

THE SYSTEM FAILS TO CONVERGE THE SYSTEM FAILS TO

CONVERGE THE SYSTEM FAILS TO CONVERGE

THE SYSTEM FAILS TO CONVERGE THE SYSTEM FAILS TO

CONVERGE THE SYSTEM FAILS TO CONVERGE

THE SYSTEM FAILS TO CONVERGE THE SYSTEM FAILS TO

CONVERGE THE SYSTEM FAILS TO CONVERGE

THE SYSTEM FAILS TO CONVERGE THE SYSTEM FAILS TO

CONVERGE THE SYSTEM FAILS TO CONVERGE

THE SYSTEM FAILS TO CONVERGE THE SYSTEM FAILS TO

CONVERGE THE SYSTEM FAILS TO CONVERGE

THE SYSTEM FAILS TO CONVERGE THE SYSTEM FAILS TO

CONVERGE THE SYSTEM FAILS TO CONVERGE

THE SYSTEM FAILS TO CONVERGE THE SYSTEM FAILS TO

CONVERGE THE SYSTEM FAILS TO CONVERGE

THE SYSTEM FAILS TO CONVERGE THE SYSTEM FAILS TO

CONVERGE THE SYSTEM FAILS TO CONVERGE

THE SYSTEM FAILS TO CONVERGE THE SYSTEM FAILS TO

CONVERGE THE SYSTEM FAILS TO CONVERGE

THE SYSTEM FAILS TO CONVERGE THE SYSTEM FAILS TO

CONVERGE THE SYSTEM FAILS TO CONVERGE

THE SYSTEM FAILS TO CONVERGE THE SYSTEM FAILS TO

CONVERGE THE SYSTEM FAILS TO CONVERGE

THE SYSTEM FAILS TO CONVERGE THE SYSTEM FAILS TO

CONVERGE THE SYSTEM FAILS TO CONVERGE

THE SYSTEM FAILS TO CONVERGE THE SYSTEM FAILS TO

CONVERGE THE SYSTEM FAILS TO CONVERGE

THE SYSTEM FAILS TO CONVERGE THE SYSTEM FAILS TO

CONVERGE THE SYSTEM FAILS TO CONVERGE

CONVERGE THE SYSTEM FAILS TO CONVERGE

THE SYSTEM FAILS TO CONVERGE THE SYSTEM FAILS TO

CONVERGE THE SYSTEM FAILS TO CONVERGE

CONVERGE THE SYSTEM FAILS TO CONVERGE

THE SYSTEM FAILS TO CONVERGE THE SYSTEM FAILS TO

About the Poet

George Abraham (they/he) is a Palestinian-American poet, writer, and Bioengineering PhD candidate at Harvard University. They are the author of two poetry chapbooks: *the specimen's apology* (Sibling Rivalry Press, 2019) and *al youm—for yesterday & her inherited traumas* (the Atlas Review, 2017). He is the recipient of fellowships from Kundiman, The Poetry Foundation, and The Watering Hole, and a member of the Radius of Arab American Writers (RAWI). He is a three-time recipient of the Favianna Rodriguez Award for Artistic Activism, and winner of the 2018 Cosmonauts Avenue Poetry Prize selected by Tommy Pico, as well as the honor of Best Poet from the College Union Poetry Slam International (CUPSI). Their writing has appeared or is forthcoming in *Tin House*, *Boston Review*, *LitHub*, *Mizna*, *The Rumpus*, *Beloit Poetry Journal*, and anthologies such as *Nepantla*, *Bettering American Poetry*, and *Beyond Memory: An Anthology of Arab American Creative Nonfiction* (University of Arkansas Press, 2019). They are currently based in Boston, where they serve as a poetry mentor for the University of Massachusetts Boston CUPSI team, and a poetry reader/ editor for *Muzzle Magazine* and the *Bettering American Poetry* anthology. Their first full-length poetry collection, *Birthright*, is forthcoming with Button Poetry in 2020.

Website: https://www.gabrahampoet.com/

Twitter: @IntifadaBatata

About the Artist

Leila Abdelrazaq is a Detroit-based Palestinian author and artist. Her debut graphic novel, *Baddawi* (Just World Books, 2015), was shortlisted for the 2015 Palestine Book Award and has been translated into three languages. She is also the author and illustrator of *The Opening* (Tosh Fesh, 2017) as well as a number of zines and short comics. Her work has been featured in *The FADER*, *The Believer Magazine*, *Harper's*, and *The Electronic Intifada*, as well as in group and solo shows in New York, Montreal, London, Beirut, and Detroit. She has given lectures and workshops on intersections of comics, activism, and self-publishing around the world. She is also the founder of Bigmouth Press & Comix.

About the Press

Sibling Rivalry Press is an independent press based in Little Rock, Arkansas. It is a sponsored project of Fractured Atlas, a nonprofit arts service organization. Contributions to support the operations of Sibling Rivalry Press are tax-deductible to the extent permitted by law, and your donations will directly assist in the publication of work that disturbs and enraptures. To contribute to the publication of more books like this one, please visit our website and click *donate*.

Sibling Rivalry Press gratefully acknowledges the following donors, without whom this book would not be possible:

Tony Taylor

Mollie Lacy

Karline Tierney

Maureen Seaton

Travis Lau

Michael Broder & Indolent Books

Robert Petersen

Jennifer Armour

Alana Smoot

Paul Romero

Julie R. Enszer

Clayton Blackstock

Tess Wilmans-Higgins & Jeff Higgins

Sarah Browning

Tina Bradley

Kai Coggin

Queer Arts Arkansas

Jim Cory

Craig Cotter

Hugh Tipping

Mark Ward

Russell Bunge

Joe Pan & Brooklyn Arts Press

Carl Lavigne

Karen Hayes

J. Andrew Goodman

Diane Greene

W. Stephen Breedlove

Ed Madden

Rob Jacques

Erik Schuckers

Sugar le Fae

John Bateman

Elizabeth Ahl

Risa Denenberg

Ron Mohring & Seven Kitchens Press

Guy Traiber

Don Cellini

John Bateman

Gustavo Hernandez

Guy Choate & Argenta Reading Series

Anonymous (12)

CPSIA information can be obtained
at www.ICGtesting.com
Printed in the USA
BVHW020000030419
544301BV00008B/62/P